My First Real Tree

♈

Jayne Relaford Brown

FootHills Publishing

Acknowledgments

Some of these poems originally appeared in the following journals and anthologies:

I Am Becoming the Woman I've Wanted (Papier-Mache): "Finding Her Here."

The Flight of the Eagle/El Vuelo del Águila (Binational Press/Editorial Binacional): "As You Fly to Chicago: A Confession," "Passing," "At Her Threshold" (as "Daughter"), "War Zone," "Before My Craving for Your Drama Waned," "A Dream of your Mother's Reluctant Blessing," "How to Live as a Lesbian Couple in the Suburbs of the U.S.A.," and "Queen Dowager's Soliloquy."

My Lover is a Woman: Contemporary Lesbian Love Poems (Ballantine): "Skylight" and "Three Songs for Touch" (as "Two Songs for Touch").

The Minnesota Review: "With Open Eyes."

Pacific Review: "Anticipation," "Anticipating Julian" and "Nearing Twelve."

Common Lives/Lesbian Lives: "Learning to Adapt."

Hurricane Alice: "Option to Renew."

Hard Love: Writings on Violence (Queen of Swords): "War Zone."

"Cusp" was originally part of a collaborative performance piece, *And Then She Kissed Me*, written and performed with Wendy Caster and Marian Thacher.

Grateful thank yous always to my three children—Morgan, Laurel, Julian—and to my life partner Janice.

ISBN: 0-941053-22-9

© Copyright 2004 Jayne Relaford Brown

Cover Artwork "Stubborn Life" by Rod MacIver
Heron Dance Art Studio and Publication
Middlebury VT   www.herondance.org

FootHills Publishing, P.O. Box 68, Kanona, NY 14856
www.foothillspublishing.com

For Janice

*Wherever you are is the "You are here"
that makes the befuddling map come clear*

CONTENTS

Light Hits Everything Along One Side

My First Real Tree	10
Firethorn, A Fairy Tale	11
Another Story	12
Housesitting for the Ex	13
Poem for a Pillbug	16
The Pit	17
Fishing	18
Queen Dowager's Soliloquy	20
Demeter's Daughters	22
"Pillar of Salt Set to Make Plunge"	23
Tendered Buttons	25
An Elemental Song	27
Cusp	28

The Green Water We've Learned to Breathe

For the Survivors	30
With Open Eyes	31
War Zone	34
Before My Craving for Your Drama Waned	36
Red Rugs	37
Love's Psychic Surgery	38
Anticipation, 1988	40
Anticipating Julian	42
Passing	43
Nearing Twelve	44
At Her Threshold	45
To My Children's Lovers	46
A Wish	48

Edenvale Avenue

Skylight	50
Learning to Adapt	52
Traveling Companion	53
Option to Renew	55
A Shady Area	56
A Dream of Your Mother's Reluctant Blessing	57
How to Live as a Lesbian Couple	
In the Suburbs of the U.S.A.	59
Possessing the Lot	60
Three Songs for Touch	61
As You Fly to Chicago, a Confession	63
Moon Swimming	65
Finding Her Here	66

LIGHT HITS EVERYTHING

ALONG ONE SIDE

♈

MY FIRST REAL TREE

Proud in my father's former shirt, my smock,
I measure white and black in every primary pint,
make the butcher paper thick
with tinted blond and gold-rust bark,
to catch a eucalyptus' branchy sweep,
its dusty green and silver leaves.

Third grade comes, a field trip
to the room that will be theirs next year.
"Gosh," one whispers. "Look what she can do!"
And this is not a lollipop I've drawn,
not the stick and circle of my youth.
It is my first real tree.
Because I've been given art to see.

"Look," Miss Desmond told us. "Not a line
across the top. The blue of sky
goes the whole way down."
        How could that be?
        The air around me's clear,
        just blue when I look up.
"Look farther out," she pointed. "See the hills?"
And then I saw it—sky reached
all the way to earth. I lived in sky!
All day long I'd spun around, tried to see
the blue I must be walking through.

I smile at those children, sight beyond
my out-held brush toward my tree.
Soon enough they'll see. This year they think
the sky is like a ceiling, still feel satisfied
with eight or sixteen crayons, have no idea
that light hits everything along one side,
that shadows huddle under fruit and basketballs,
that everything converges, disappears
in one small dot at the world's edge.

FIRETHORN, A FAIRY TALE

You hold a rose-red pippin up,
press the apple to your cheek,
peer at me and slyly wink.

These very fingers, traced with moon,
two dozen years ago drew back the drapes
in the old house behind the thorny hedge.

You watched me as I ran home, late,
and risked the shortcut through
your orchard's reaching branches.

Did you watch, as well,
the night a little prince of twelve
kissed me beneath your apple trees?
I gave my bike away, and fell
asleep what seems a hundred years.

A dozen dashing princes came
to wake me with their kiss.
I lay there being beautiful and pale,
unmoved upon my pallet.

They marked the sudden color
of my cheek as promise.
Oh, but my mind burned
with pyracantha at its base,
a wild forest of firethorn
draped with heavy maidenhair.

Still and stubborn, I slept on,
till you in your dark disguise
drew near, drew back your hood,
and silver hair fell wild to your waist.

You rubbed mandragora at my wrists,
sighed, "Ah, my golden delicious,"
and woke me, with sweet
white apple at my lips.

ANOTHER STORY

This is not the story of a family steadily, togetherly
plucked from dirt farm, via war, to opportunity,
up the rung-by-rung of the corporate you-know-what
to the nice suburban home, four bright kids with braces,
sterling grades and manners, lovely Methodists.
That's her parents' story.

It's not even the story behind the story,
the lies told to the nice Methodists
like "I was at the after-prom" instead of
"I was swimming in the ocean high on mescaline
inside the full moon's trough,"
or getting caught in Spanish lab
with Gertrude Stein behind the dialogues—
"¿Donde está la biblioteca?"
The nonplussed Spanish teacher asked,
"Do you understand this?"
"I don't know," she answered, meaning it.

Because this *is* the story of "I don't know"—
the next generation caught like a pendulum,
a bobble-headed dashboard doll, between
the fear of repetition and the gaping hole.
A story of fits and starts, half-planned,
half-raised families, half-assed plans
for who we'd be when we grow up.
The story of a nice Methodist anarchist,
a staggered dreamer trying lives like outfits
till she sees there's nothing left to wear,
and stands there naked in a house just like her parents'
—only rented.

HOUSESITTING FOR THE EX

i.   HOW TO SLEEP WITHIN HER WALLS

Draw skin in close.
       Tuck extra flesh between
              your legs and under arms.
Hunch neck.
       Keep windows open:
              clear your head.
Sleep with covers to your neck.

What a move, to get me here!
It seemed at first
       like such an overture
              to being friends again:
"Here, come and stay a week or so
while I'm in Rome.
If you'd just feed the cat
and brush her once a day for fleas,
then you could sleep here, and enjoy the beach.
I crush them in between my thumbnail
and the comb, but you can drown them
just as easily in alcohol.
With water, they keep swimming to the top—"

And then: "—I'd rather you don't use
the better china. But if you'd like,
you may borrow my old bike."

ii.   HOW TO BRING HER DOWN TO SIZE

Lift cushions up to see
       the dust and hair,
find her pricey crackers stale,
       her olive oil rancid.
Diagnose the things she's chosen
       to surround herself.

Lift your nostrils
        at the mothball breath
that kills the odor
        of her cedar chest.
See how the porcelain she loves
        in cool green celadon
is interspersed on shelves with florid
        wooden snakes and birds.

Note her stiff-backed furniture,
        her penchant for cymbidiums
that would have left
        O'Keeffe aghast.

iii.   WHAT YOU HAVE THAT SHE DOES NOT

Invite your lover here.
Tease-touch with fingertips
until she's cried your name
        more often than
              the pastel walls can drink,
        louder than
              the lamb's wool carpets can absorb.

Close the windows:
        let it fill her house.

And when your lover curls to you
        and sleeps, gently disengage,
and walk the house.
        Stroke porcelain.
            Crush an orchid
        with your thumbs,
slip it in
        between her china plates.

This will be enough:
       when she returns, your name
              will drum its presence in her ears.
She'll lie awake at night
       as though she's in a stranger's bed,
             grow drowsy in the afternoons
      and dream she's naked, standing
           at her open windows,
                   crying out your name.

POEM FOR A PILLBUG

Sowbug, pillbug, roly-poly,
bibblebug, my little monkey pea—
so cute it took so long to see
the way you gnawed at me.

You rolled into a little ball
at even my most gentle touch.
Your tender parts shrunk out of reach
behind those plates, away from me.

Did you see me as enemy?
Twirling you within my palm,
you struck me so with empathy
for your defenseless stance from me

that, hoping I could coax you free,
I spent whole hours motionless.
When I could be as still as death,
you'd grant your tickling gift to me.

And then I started noticing
my cucurbits had disappeared,
my pansies had their faces sheared,
their stems were bit to ragged things.

At blossom's base, you ate your fill.
You sensed me near, and rolled up quick
but, unimpressed, I gave a flick,
and sent you tumbling, little pill.

Sowbug, pillbug, wood louse, monkey pea—
Don't come crawling back to eat
this tenderness. Your strategy
no longer tickles me.

THE PIT

You stand at the bottom of a crater,
the huge hole that shows your hurt.
I look down from its lip.

"Okay," you say,
"Throw down your love."
I toss some in,
and you cry back,
"Oh honey, that won't do.
You can't fill
this hole with that!"

I throw in more,
            and more,
and you compact it
with your feet,
stamp it down
until it seems
like nothing's changed.
You call my love "inadequate."

I gather up the last I have
and throw it at you, hard.
It sends you tumbling
in your pit.

"Hey," you say,
as you struggle to stand,
"what the hell was that?"

"Love," I answer,
and dust my hands.

And as I leave, I hear your work:
the repeated ring of pick on rock.

FISHING

Will I look up to see
you look at me one day,
your eyes gone hard
like you'd mistaken me
for someone else,
and wondered how I'd come
to occupy your chair, your house,
to bring my fleshy self,
that snot, those smells,
that flannel robe half-open,
like I thought I might have
something you would want?

        Bodies flashing silver light,
        they surge together overhead.
        Here and there I see a fin
        slipped through the threads,
        bright backlit fans,
        the panicked spread of tiny ribs,
        and then those roundest,
        deepest eyes look down,
        just before the net's collapse.

Or will it go the other way:
the scales go dry, fall from my eyes
like a net torn through,
and I'll see nothing
but the ragged tooth of you?
Your voice will be a grate
old anecdotes sift through.
I'll realize I've memorized
your repertoire, that where my nerves
once thrilled for you is still.

        Sterling bodies plunge for me,
        the flip of muscle slick down breasts,
        belly, thighs, they dive to kiss my toes.

They flop about my feet, contort and reach.
Their bright coins scatter
on the deck and dry to grey.
A wicked stink as muscle spasms still,
and the last round eye
gives up its shine.

QUEEN DOWAGER'S SOLILOQUY
*for Hobie, and Padric,
and for John, who is gone*

You should have seen me at the bar last night!
Two hours before they kicked me out,
and Michael even introducing me
        as Duchess So-and-So.

No, not Windsor, dear, but close.
Seriously, thank you for the blouse.
I wish you'd borrow the silk kimono
when you throw your Christmas bash.

It was so kind of you
to include me in your holidays.
I've bought presents for the kids
and I promise I'll behave—

lower my voice and all,
and keep a stiff upper wrist.
I wish you could have seen me, though.

Oh, do you suppose I could borrow
your black jacket tomorrow?
Now it's John that's gone, poor boy.

God, I'm sick of funerals!
It's just so odd—I've wept
into my beer for years

because no one wants
an old queen with sagging jowls
and bags below the eyes.

And now these cute young boys
are dying in droves.
And I'm alive.

Celibate against my will,
God knows—
but I'm alive.

And who knows,
it could be years
before cirrhosis does me in.

Anyway, thanks for the cocoa.
Give the kids a kiss for me.
I really must go—
Happy Hour, you know.

DEMETER'S DAUGHTERS
to Dorothy Jayne

When Demeter's daughter
was stolen away,
the goddess made the planet
answer for her loss:
struck trees leafless,
withered crops,
killed cattle, all the world
stilled, stunned,
frozen with maternal grief.

When Dorothy's daughter sank from sight
into the mind's dank underground,
Dorothy stole a few long lunch hours,
cried behind the filing cabinet at work,
searched out the latest books
on herbal cures to retrieve the lost.

She tended to her daughter's body:
took away its cigarettes,
spread aloe vera on its burns,
sent it bowling once a week,
drove it to the clinic Tuesdays,
rubbed its back until it fell asleep.

She tended to that husk
until it rose again,
returned to school to graduate,
where Dorothy caused some talk
with the torrents of her tears,
the bloom along her cheek,
the dimples springing up
behind the clicking camera.

Demeter ruled a goddess's domain.
All that's left her daughters is interior terrain.
    But Dorothy's world suffered
    with its winter just the same.

"PILLAR OF SALT SET TO MAKE PLUNGE"
--Associated Press, Jerusalem

There is no doubt the pillar will fall.
Geologists blame the interplay
    of salt, stone and rain.
        "But if it's nature,
            I can't really complain,"

said a ranger who surveyed the shift
in Mt. Sodom's forty-five foot high
    tourist attraction.
        The spire was not asked
            for her reaction.

Flee for your life; do not look back.
Flee to the hills, lest you be consumed.
    What might have consumed
        her, walking behind him
            past their poor friends, doomed?

Following *him* who had just offered
their two daughters to an angry mob.
    He, so quick to trade
        their children
            and the life they'd made,

just to rescue these two sudden guests,
then, on their word, had made her gather
    up their girls, and run,
        without good-byes, with
            no home, once again.

Was it any wonder she looked back?
Or was there more? Could she have leaned
    toward Sodom and Gomorrah's ways,
        turned in hopes to catch
            a certain eye's last gaze?

The pillar's leaned more rapidly
toward the abyss in recent months.
     Is there life in lime,
           slow, but sentient? Making
                 up your mind takes time.

TENDERED BUTTONS
--A thank you letter to Gertrude Stein

In eras when we couldn't utter "Clitoris"
or kiss another of a gender homogenous,
I wonder if I could have found
the hooded words you smuggled in.

Tender words to women,
       tiny, tough,
to roll around the mouth,
to slide the tongue across
and pocket in discreet cheeks.

Hard-headed on hairy tweed
or smooth and slick as pearls,
words to roll and worry
in the palm to soothe,
to rub against in solitude.

Mostly chosen to match fabric,
those aware of buttons know.
Mostly, most are mostly unaware.

I wonder, Gertrude, if you'd like
the ways we are today.
We own our own parades and presses,
although the main continues to oppress us.
Wait—I want to say:
       Although the main continues to oppress us,
         we own our own parades and presses.

What I'm saying, Gertrude,
is even now we need your words.
Openness is circular.
In eras when we wear our buttons
bright and very there,
those who'd never think of buttons,
they begin to be aware,

of being scared, of feeling
less-than-rare. They begin to care
that we are there.

But you and Alice give us cause
to celebrate, for now,
and courage for those days
when we might choose to choose
our buttons carefully, to blend.
But even then, like you,
to raise them up enough
that those who seek such buttons
find them by their touch.

AN ELEMENTAL SONG

Will you be the hurricane of my own making,
wet winds swirled from my fingers?
Will you be the earth of my own making,
canyons that collapse around old angers,
granting me your shudder and release?

Will I be the pot of your own turning,
raw porcelain that opens at your touch?
Enter at the center of my yearning,
thin my spinning walls and see how much
capacity I hold within my cup.

Be the rising blaze of my own burning,
molten heat that bubbles through the crust.
Bring your tinder, conjure
coals I've let be muffled under dust.
Blow away the ash that covers passion.
Breathe, until the flames lick up and catch.
Be my wick and friction. Be my match.

CUSP

It's the edge of a tooth
or a crucial place
where a curving journey
meets itself,

the moment of movement
out of a house, a fold or flap
in the valve of a heart,
the tip of the moon,

it's the point in a turn
when a skater shifts
on the edge of her blade.

Ride out the turn,
savor the tooth,
open the chamber,
don't be afraid.

THE GREEN WATER

WE'VE LEARNED TO BREATHE

♈

FOR THE SURVIVORS

How we do it—rise from the mire
and muck, the suck of the past,
while algae and grasses, heavy epaulettes,
drape our shoulders, drag us back:

We lift ourselves from the silt-bottomed lake,
reeds snagging our reach for the promising air.
As we blink in the day's large light,
water still pulls at us, clamorous,
soothing as sleep.

We stand, try to stand
our spotlit selves, our mucky stink,
then dip again into the drink,
as if we could wash in filthy water,
leave what belongs in the clotted lake,
and come out clean.

The silt slope slips beneath our feet,
and we surrender to its downward drift.
Toes stretch in memory's cool mud,
and the cut, from tin lid or bottle's broken neck,
never fails to surprise us,
though it never fails.

We salve the wounds with bottom-mud,
stop up our ears and mouths
with the green water we've learned to breathe.
Dead-Man's Float is a kind of rest
when familiar currents jostle us.

And yet, and then, we begin again,
to lift, to push from that old sweet ooze,
rise through the lovely, deadly wet,
and choose instead the hard, sharp air.

WITH OPEN EYES

i.
The winner grinned at me,
said "thank you"
as he zipped his pants.
There was a window to the right.
I learned to look right through
so if they didn't speak—
the others didn't speak—
I could just wait
till they were through,
and almost be alone.

They told me white girl hippies
swallow anything,
but I was grateful for their drugs—
the same numb
that meant I couldn't run
meant I couldn't feel them
touching me.

I lived that night
by listing what I saw
beyond the frame—
Moon, Tree, Cloud, Car—
then shutting up my eyes
to memorize the names.

Moon. Tree. Cloud Car.
Moon, who shines soft on me.
Tree, I could climb
Cloud, that could hide me.
Car, that could drive me
away from that room.

ii.
Sometimes since, I've tried to look,

and found a stranger
with his eyes rolled back,
turned inward, focused on
his own thrust into space,
the empty space
I'd left for him.

Sometimes I've found
that gaze again,
the one I saw before
I thought to look away
into the window's frame:
intense precision peering
like a hunter down his sights
just before the trigger squeeze.

With my closed eyes,
one lover thought me passionate,
transported by his skill.
Another screamed at me to look.
She knew she wasn't holding me.
I whispered "Moon" and ran.

iii.
Twenty years, and still,
I turn my head just right,
my cheek against the sheet
the way it was that night,
I close my eyes and whisper
"MoonTreeCloudCar,
MoonTreeCloudCar,"
 and climb, crying "Moon,"
through the window again
to the place
I can't
be touched.

I want to watch your eyes,
but learned too long ago to hide
But sometimes, when your fingers,
tender, draw me toward the comfort
of your cupped hand's nest,
I nestle down, surprise myself
with a new desire—

I imagine I could look one day,
and find your eyes
so softly seeing me,
the way they'd wait
with such a gentle watch,
asking how to better touch,

and how they'd brighten
when I reach to cup your cheek
and whisper, "Moon—
Moon, who shines so soft."

WAR ZONE

For a moment I was there with you,
the night I woke up, trapped.
You covered every inch of me
and pinned me to the bed.
Your heart a burst of fire
at my ribs, you hid me
from the planes you saw.

I'd stroke your hair
and whisper, "It's okay, okay now,"
but you thrashed your legs
and cried as though
the covers buried you.

Once I woke to find you
crawling through the house.
You heard me, leapt, and raised
a butcher knife, your blank eyes
in some other country, other year,
before they rolled back
and you fell toward sleep.

You slid your way around
the edges of our rooms,
kept your back from me
against a solid wall.
You saw me dart my eyes
toward the door to go,
began to pin me to the bed,
the wall, the floor,
to save your life
instead of mine.

I learned to take a corner of the bed,
avoid the bruises when I could.
You told me once you feel
so guilty you survived.

I start to understand.
I finally left a note for you:
"There is no winning   to this war,"
left you crawling through your dreams
so I could sleep in peace.

BEFORE MY CRAVING FOR YOUR DRAMA WANED

Locked in my new studio, I wait.
The deadbolt's turned, and food
and water stocked for seven days.

I crouch beside the windowsill,
scan the street toward your house
and guess which headlights might be yours.

The second day at noon I ask
my neighbor down the hall
to check the parking lot.

"All clear," he calls, and says he might
have seen you by my car last night.
But he's a gossip. I can't count on that.

You never came for me and knocked
my door down, tried to take me back.
Just once you called and told me,

"This is stupid. Get back home
where you belong." I'd taped a note
across the phone: *Be strong, be strong.*

"No," I said. "This time I mean it.
Don't call back." I hung the phone up
over taped-on words, and waited for your ring,

your knuckles rapping at my door,
your searching voice that always set
my heart to thumping in its sack.

RED RUGS

Red rugs hide blood, but the shag
still stiffens underfoot.
Would you like a tour of the house?

I've covered everything in plastic since,
kept it just the same
while I try to reconstruct.

I think he dragged me down this hall,
and that flower vase was broken
as he pulled me past.

See, three hairs of mine have caught
in this blossom of dried artichoke.
He must have called for others then,

a dozen came—see how
the carpet's matted here?—
held hypodermics, needle up,

squeezed, until a single,
sticky drop eased out
and trembled at the tip.

I looked just once.
One grinned at me—a wet
front tooth that glistened gold.

I rolled my face away, stared past
the sliding glass at the helpless moon
till they were done.

One of my back molars
broke in half last week.
I've come to like

the way my tongue
fits in that empty
rasping place.

LOVE'S PSYCHIC SURGERY

We lock our eyes
and reach, and freeze.
Behind the walls
of gristled bone
we pull up short
at the fragile sack
and grasp its beat.

We've traded caution
for a window glimpsed
within the other's eye.
Giving trust a final try,
we grant the power to break
through bone and flesh,
power to heal, to kill, to cure.

Faced off like this,
hands to elbows
in each other's chests,
for one of us
to shift now
could mean death.

I didn't want
to feel my hand
surround your heart,
its spill that over-
laps my palm,
the way I cup
to take it up
and know just where
my nails could tear.

Don't trust this hand
that's never learned
the firm and steady
grasp you seek,

these fingers likely,
when they feel this weight,
to clasp too tight,
or back away
and drop this gift.

And now your grasp
has made me feel
forgotten want,
my stubborn beat.

I pulse within your fist,
forced to know
I like this press.

So much so,
if you must pull back,
I'd rather have you
rip it out,
and not be left
to feel its reach,
its rattle in
my empty chest.

ANTICIPATION, 1988

I count my children every night,
sleep best between their crush
of heavy, restless limbs,
our blankets spread across the floor,
close to ground as possible.

Twice this fall, I've waked
to crazy, pitching walls,
run numbly to my children
in their beds,
and gathered them
inside the hall.

The quake stops at last.
We laugh, and talk too loud,
turn on the radio
to quantify
that endless, empty roar.

And so I wait,
for the Great Quake
they claim is overdue.
I jump at any sudden noise.
I always do,

because in no less dread, I wait
for the strange plane at the horizon
which becomes a squadron,
the creak along the hall
that finally is the killer's footfall,
the bark of backfired car,
the fireworks that kill—
that white and final flash.

It's not what form
the armegeddon takes,
but that we're separate.

So I sleep best with them
in bed with me, in reach,
or prowl their rooms
and plan my routes

to run to them
in case we get
that second's chance—
a last embrace.

ANTICIPATING JULIAN

I float, a light, translucent
Disneyland balloon,
your beaming face inside
more real than I.

My little character,
I'm a bubble of waiting,
a pregnant pause,
a nine-moon madonna.

I imagine you, my little buddha,
in perfect lotus posture
as I come to terms
with your arrival.

This strange serenity,
to disregard reports of risk—
to be untroubled you refuse to turn.
You seem deliberate in this.

My sweet beatitude,
blond breech of promise,
I love you first
for refusing gravity.

PASSING

"You don't know what it's like,"
she says, "to feel ashamed,
like I can't bring my friends in here,
afraid they'll figure out
my mother's gay
and think I'm weird."

Once, I carried cookies
to her fourth-grade class,
a plate of frosted hearts
my passport back
into the world I'd left.

A teacher passing by
beamed pleasantly at me.
The principal winked—
"Looks great," he said.
I ate approval up,
a hunger I'd forgot I had.

I wished then I could
laminate that plate,
fake it, carry cookies
every day, seem sweet
as needed, gather up
those smiles like bouquets.

"You don't know what it's like,"
she said, "to want to live
like normal people do.
You don't know how I feel."

I meet her swimming eyes.
"Yes I do," I say,
and no, I've no idea."
Neither answer's right.
She bites her fist
and turns her face.

NEARING TWELVE
(1986)

Behind our house,
uncut head lettuce
presses skyward,
blown to seed.
Not caught in time,
       inedible,
a bitter, awkward weed.

Behind your door,
you measure yourself
against me daily.
A single pencil stroke
for me floats just above
your hundred rising marks.

Beyond my bedroom wall, you sleep,
mouth open, head thrown back,
new breasts pressed against pastel sheets.
Your heavy blonde hair
darkens by the day.
Tangled blankets strangle limbs.
You throw the covers off,
turn and toss against my wall.
Thunder strikes me,
       startled, from my sleep.

AT HER THRESHOLD

When I wore skirts, she held them out like wings,
then closed herself inside to disappear,
her head between my thighs, or held her cheek
against my belly while I stroked her hair.

We two were tethered long beyond the break
of nature's actual coiled cord. In sleep
she sought my body, wriggled in between
and pushed her father out, to feel my heart.

I'd taught her how to sleep on me like that
and feel the beat she'd grown accustomed to,
until she grew too long for me to bear.
"You're heavy now. Get off. This has to stop."

Now I reach to hold her and she draws away
as though she thought I'd meant to pull her down.
She swims some place inside her hardened skin
where I can't reach, where I won't be allowed.

Now each night's "I love you" sinks unanswered down
beneath her deep resentment's murky pond,
while I stand foolish at its edge and wait
in case one day she'll ferry me across.

"Well, sweet dreams, then."
                                      Close the bedroom door
and seek the haven that she hates me for:
the one who lets me sleep against her heart,
and strokes my back until it stills the hurt.

TO MY CHILDREN'S LOVERS

I feel such violence, such tenderness, toward you.
You've made my children pink as pups.
They tumble toward you,
joyous, whimpering,
in bodies once again outsized,
new as when they first stepped out
from couch and coffee table, tottered
toward my inheld breath, my outheld arms.

You will catch them, you will let them fall.
They dance for you now—"Look at me!"
—they try their skits, their magic tricks, on you.
Your clapping hands, your smile or kiss
are manna to them now; your frown, your yawn,
your glance away, can kill.

I'd hate you, but you look so much like me.
The way you move, ambivalent,
in bodies you can halfway understand
are both your power and your curse,
you could be my daughters, or myself.
You gleam and smolder near my children
like I beamed toward their father once,
and I am so afraid of how that light can fade.

You've come to these relationships
as new and wounded as my kids.
You each reach out and clutch the way
the almost-drowned take down the rescuer.

When baby bodies trusted me,
I always slid my hand
between the diaper and their skin.
I took the pin's quick stick,
and would have died
before I'd hurt them. But I did, I did.

"No one else will ever
get that close," they'd swear to me.
Now they fling away the exoskeletons
of cool it took them years to mold.
Like crutch-tossers at Lourdes
they rise from mildewed cots and dance,
giddy to be saved.
I want to shake you: "Listen!
Do you see the damage you could do?"

And yet, in taking them, you give them back.
Generous in joy, in hurt, they quiz me on my past—
       "How can you tell when you're falling in love?"
       "Have you loved someone you couldn't trust?"—
as if what I'd lived through was a legacy
as much as olive skin or allergies to bees.

In their infancy as lovers, they *talk* to me again,
let me take them in my arms, and feel
the holding with no holding back
we haven't known in years.
       Even as I curse you for their pain,
       I'm thanking you for that.

A WISH

If we could all be two and timeless,
travel back and take us in our arms,

say the words we needed, hold ourselves.
If we could, we could have told ourselves,

"You've done enough," kissed our cheeks,
and whispered, "Rest now. Rest."

EDENVALE AVENUE

♈

SKYLIGHT

Lie here, you say.
The clouds are sailing by.
The wind's picked up.

Careful not to touch,
I stretch along your body,
place my head a fraction
of an inch from yours

inside the small square
of light-charged air
that heats your comforter.

Look up, you murmur.
See the way they slide?
I watch, grow dizzy
with the pace

as white silks slip
across the turquoise frame,
as your cool breath
moves moist against my ear.

This is where I love
to lie and dream, you say.
And here's the moment
I could tell you

I've been dreaming too,
    of you,
or simply turn my face
and meet your lips,

the moment I could trust
I understand your hints,
and why you've brought me
    to this place.

And if I kissed you
softly as a cloud,
traveled over you
as slowly as a mist,

and entered you
as gentle as a fog,
would I be
as welcome as a rain?

Would you lie still,
watch sky as if
I wasn't touching you?
Would you run?

Or would you sigh,
so glad to finally
have the waiting done,
and turn to me?

And, like a storm,
could we, together,
gather?

LEARNING TO ADAPT

You have to understand,
this is pretty damn confusing.
When you began to leave those notes
—and roses!—on my car,
and I found you waiting
outside a three-hour seminar
just to be with me,
I thought, oh shit.

And when I said,
"You're coming on
too strong. I'm scared,"
you said, "We'll take it
at your pace," and sent me iris
wreathed in baby's breath.

And when I turned
away from you
to button up my jeans,
afraid you'd finally see
my sagging belly
in the light,
you turned me to you,
blessed it with a kiss.

Be patient, please.
I could get used to this.

TRAVELING COMPANION

"Love—the last frontier,"
I used to say.
Sometimes I meant it
more like outer space, unreachable.

I thought of it more often
as a foreign place:
a land too wild for my taste,
too treacherous at best.
I loved the colorful brochures,
but heard of people
who had traveled there
and disappeared.

I'd only visited, a tourist's
whirlwind, contained.
Just enough experience
so I could say,
        "Oh yeah,
        it's pretty primitive.
        Sure, the food is great,
        if you don't get sick."

What drew me first—
what let me stay—
was finding someone else
who felt as lost
and out of place.

Unaccustomed as we were
to love-talk's liquid syllables,
we improvised our own,
a polyglot of tenderness
and nerves, a double-leveled lexicon
with single words that said:
        Come here, but not too close.
        Ignore that. Yes, I'm scared,

but it's delicious to move past.

In every foreign station
we pass through,
our words are oars in open air.

We stretch, and learn a unison,
grow fluent in this pull together
into deeper inner space.

When did this travel
start to feel like home?

I've let you crash
past every border,
rib and gristle,
I'd spent decades
staking up,

and moved with you
into these heartlands
where each of us composes
territory, traveler, and base.

OPTION TO RENEW

Thirty days by thirty days
we make this rented house a home.
I claim the grounds by what I plant.

Tenuous and quick, purple sweet peas
mark new boundaries, race
to cover fences made of string.

Orange poppies open, fall,
toss offspring through the yard,
and rise again from woody stems.

What we make of us—
this house, each other—
we take bit by bit.

I won't plant trees—
we don't have promises that long—
but I invest in seeds.

I don't know where it leads,
this shared experiment.
I hope you're strong enough to stay.

You are the first
whose love I count in years
to whom I hurry home.

A SHADY AREA

Watering today, I thought about
the afternoon we chose this place.
The landlord handed me a pink camellia,
bowed and kissed my hand,
charming me to rent from him, I guess.

He didn't see me lay the blossom
on your thigh inside the car,
or brush its petals at your breast
once we had cleared the drive.

I thought I'd be less hidden
once we got the papers signed.
Let him try to throw us out!
Like these stunted sweet pea stalks
I planted north of the eugenia hedge,
I thought about the props,
forgot about the necessary light

And when he saw our second bedroom
crammed with desks and bookcases,
and asked, "Where will you sleep?"
I shrunk in my resolve.
"I have a bed for sale," he said.
"It's cheap."

                    I didn't speak.
I told myself we needed
curtains in the den,
a shower head replaced,
and what's the point
of having landlords
on your case?

A DREAM OF YOUR MOTHER'S RELUCTANT BLESSING

This is not the fear dream
where she keeps the car warm
while your father pushes
down our door to kidnap you.

Not the one in which
you write a letter,
get a telegram
she's had a stroke
as her response.

Not the nightmare
where the hospital
calls them, not me,
to say you've died.

In this fantasy,
your mom and I
sit side by side.
Our wide thighs touch,
her photo albums fan
across our laps.

She points to snapshots—
second in a line of girls,
you fidget in your Easter dress
and scratch your leg, holding
"O" for "MOTHER" cockeyed
in your other hand.

"She couldn't stand to try on clothes,"
your mother says. "To hold her long enough
to pin a hem was pure hell
for both of us.

I touch the picture where you grip

your hockey stick, smile and say,
"She's still like that."

A shadow moves behind her eyes.
She plumbs my face, and makes a choice.
"Let me comb your hair," she says.
She pats the floor between her knees.
"Shall I call you 'daughter,' dear,"
she asks, "or what?" She tugs my hair
and plaits two screaming lines
against my scalp as I sit motionless,
a test, then pats my back.

We're cronies in this dream,
your mom and I,
if not by choice—
the only two who know
you sleep best
when we rub your neck,
who lift your hair to kiss
the rosy birthmark at the nape,
who gauge your anger
by your temple's vein,
your fear by one curled hand,
 kept hidden in your lap.

HOW TO LIVE AS A LESBIAN COUPLE IN THE SUBURBS OF THE U.S.A.

From chicken wire, newsprint, paste,
build up a slathered, hardened skin.
Hang it up, and crawl inside
this thin encasement for your place.

Pretend you're all alone and safe,
nobody cares there's bending wrists,
and sighs, or how your fingers trace
each other's sweets, unwrap them, lick.

And if you like this pretty dream,
but wake to find a stick has ripped
your walls apart, and thrown you down
along with all your treats and tricks,

in front of blindfold men with bats,
a laughing crowd that waits to jump,
just cover up and take your lumps,
make paste, tear strips of print, repeat.

POSSESSING THE LOT

My anniversary gift from you:
a rake with eight-inch teeth.
I squat among the lettuces
with water jugs, and send
my matching consort cats
to kill the grasshoppers
that chomp and shit
among my tender leaves.

You've said the only thing
you wish for us is peace.
I've done my best.
You'll be surprised when you return.

I've dug a ditch around our yard,
buried rows of crystal points,
obsidian and amethysts.

I'm growing golden sage and rue
to smoke the noisy neighbors out.
I've asked the eucalyptus trees
to root, and rout their houses up.

Our two cats bat a lizard out
from underneath the compost heap.
I cultivate my sage and wait
until this house will stand alone,
a tract of one among the trees.

The road will shrivel to a path
all set about with treacherous thorns,
the owners will forget the way,
the bees, the cats, and I will hum,
and wait for your return.

THREE SONGS FOR TOUCH

i.   SKIN

Hands to cup a chin and cheek,
lips to trace a nape of neck.

Hips to fit a belly's curve,
words to witness what we have.

I used to say *A pillow pressed
against my chest will pass for touch.*

But now to press along your back,
reach over you and cup your breast—

I'll never know a better rest.

ii.   SLEEPING WITH YOU

Tenderest: soft stroked cheek
        beside my breast,
my kiss there, then you stretch.

Your palm supports my neck
        and I remember how
to let the body rest,
        to trust this willingness.

You tug on me as surely
        as a newborn's suck
knots up the womb again,
        beloved draw that rakes
            and heals old emptiness.

iii.   MY LOVER'S HAIR

Love, your hair
smells chocolate tonight,
and sugar and cinnamon
caught as you bent
at the hot oven door.

Sweetmeat, fine feast—
spooned against you,
the bowl of my body,
the cup of my life,
brims with your spice.

AS YOU FLY TO CHICAGO, A CONFESSION

Before you left, I bought another chain
so your quartz ornament could pendant down
between your breasts and weight the hollow place
I like to lay my hand to calm your breath.

I know I often give you what I need.
And now you're gone, and I'm a wishbone sprung,
an unhinged sternum with its ribs all slipped
and disengaged, the flopping heart uncaged.

I wander like I'm lost around our house,
from desk to yard to empty bed and back—
which means the joke's on me when I admit
that I could hardly wait for you to leave.

I pictured part of me who would emerge
in solitude: the hard-edged writer grown
too flaccid from the comforts of your love,
who longed to keen and howl about the house

and rattle back to skeletal remains
of pain's incisive, easy eloquence,
instead of groping to articulate
the brinkless, sloppy liquid of our love.

Janice, remember diagrams we drew
in grade school, shading in to show how deep
two circles intersect? I'm scared to find
how far you've cast yourself across my life.

If our relationship is like two spheres
that deeply overlap, am I eclipsed,
the part that's "us" what love has pencilled in,
so when you leave I'm like a bitten moon?

We both run cringing at the sound of "Wife,"
its spectre draped with aprons, dresses, men.

But I need words to show I mean to stay,
to say how very deep in me you spin.

Fly back to me, and lay your palm against
this heart that spills itself in search of you.
Your hand completes the line that marks my edge
and lets me recognize my life's own breath.

MOON SWIMMING

Wait by the pool for a Strawberry Moon
and catch the change—pale blues that deepen
to an indigo, how Venus flickers first,
then the Dipper's ladle in the West,
as though it spills the day's last light.
You've thought of night as if
the planetarium dropped in a different slide.
Tonight you know these stars
burn constant in the sky.

Turn east to watch the gathered glow,
to guess the place the moon will lift.
A thin girl in an upstairs window looks
beyond you for the planet-star,
her lank hair an auburn curtain by her face,
mirror to the limp lace she's pushed aside
to catch tonight's first glance, and make her wish.

Inside the house, your lover lights a lamp,
lies down to read, will later move to make
a place for you within that circle's warmth.

But now the coalescence has begun.
Mockingbirds and crickets hush. Moon's rising—no,
your world's spun to bring you to its view.
Full-bellied orange at foothills' line
before the paler faces—butter, pearl—beam,
and blue light spills its satin sheen across your feet.

To make it rise on you again, duck down below
the notched horizon of the redwood fence.
Sit at the water's lip, tuck moon-kissed legs
into the night-black pool, slide off your dress
and slip into the cool black basin's drift.
Float, your arms and legs outstretched,
a star yourself, a constellation, globes
of milky breasts, of belly, knees,
wait, water-lapped, to echo back reflected light.

FINDING HER HERE

I am becoming the woman I've wanted,
grey at the temples,
soft body, delighted,
cracked up by life
with a laugh that's known bitter,
but, past it, got better,
knows she's a survivor—
that whatever comes,
she can outlast it.
I am becoming a deep
       weathered basket.

I am becoming the woman I've longed for,
the motherly lover
with arms strong and tender,
the growing-up daughter
who blushes surprises.
I am becoming full moons
       and sunrises.

I find her becoming,
this woman I've wanted,
who knows she'll encompass,
who knows she's sufficient,
knows where she's going
and travels with passion.
Who remembers she's precious,
yet not at all scarce—
who knows she is plenty,
       plenty to share.

♈